DK EYEWITNESS WORKBOOKS
Stars & Planets

by Claire Watts

Educational Consultants Linda B. Gambrell
and Geraldine Taylor

Project Editors Clare Hibbert, Sue Malyan
Senior Editors Jane Yorke, Fleur Star
Senior Art Editor Owen Peyton Jones
Editors Nayan Keshan, Mark Silas
US Editor Lori Cates Hand
Art Editors Sara Nunan, Peter Radcliffe, Tanisha Mandal
DK Picture Library Claire Bowers, Rose Horridge
Managing Editors Christine Stroyan, Shikha Kulkarni
Managing Art Editors Anna Hall, Govind Mittal
DTP Designers Siu Chan, Andy Hilliard, Ronaldo Julien, Anita
Yadav, Tanveer Zaidi
Production Editor Tom Morse
Production Controller Nancy-Jane Maun
Senior Jacket Designer Suhita Dharamjit
Jacket Design Development Manager Sophia MTT
Publisher Andrew Macintyre
Art Director Karen Self
Publishing Director Jonathan Metcalf

This American Edition, 2020
First American Edition, 2008
Published in the United States by DK Publishing
1450 Broadway, Suite 801, New York, NY 10018

A catalog record for this book
is available from the Library of Congress.
ISBN: 978-0-7440-3456-1

DK books are available at special discounts when purchased in bulk
for sales promotions, premiums, fund-raising, or educational use.
For details, contact: DK Publishing Special Markets, 1450 Broadway,
Suite 801, New York, NY 10018
SpecialSales@dk.com

Printed and bound in Canada

For the curious

www.dk.com

Contents

Fast Facts

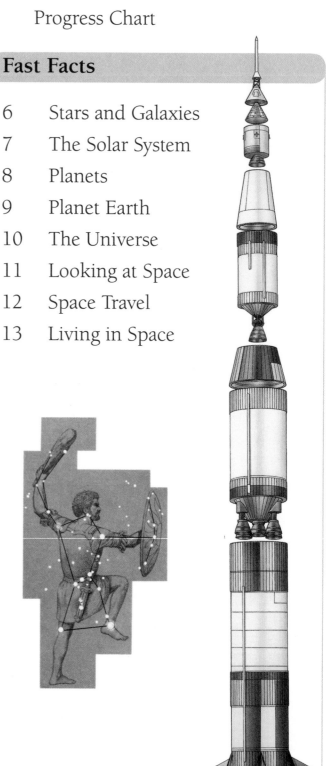

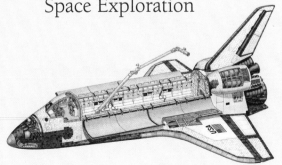

How This Book Can Help Your Child

The Eyewitness Workbooks series offers a fun and colorful range of stimulating titles in the subjects of history, science, and geography. Devised and written with the expert advice of educational consultants, each workbook aims to:

- develop a child's knowledge of a popular topic
- provide practice of key skills and reinforce classroom learning
- nurture a child's special interest in a subject.

About This Book

Eyewitness Workbook Stars & Planets is an activity-packed exploration of the world of space and astronomy. Inside you will find:

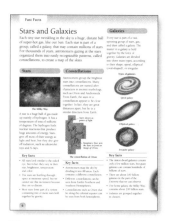

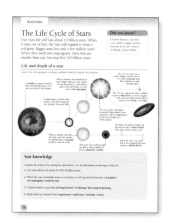

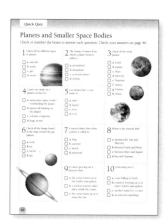

Fast Facts

This section presents key information as concise facts, which are easy to digest, learn, and remember. Encourage your child to start by reading through the valuable information in the Fast Facts section and studying the statistics charts at the back of the book before trying out the activities.

Activities

The enjoyable fill-in activities are designed to develop information recall and help your child practice cross-referencing skills. Each activity can be completed using information provided on the page, in the Fast Facts section, or on the charts at the back of the book.

Quick Quiz

There are six pages of multiple-choice questions to test your child's newfound knowledge of the subject. Children should try answering the quiz questions only after all of the activity section has been completed.

Important Information

- Please stress to your child the importance of heeding the warnings in this book. Never look directly at the Sun or try to view it using a telescope, binoculars, or a mirror. Only view a solar eclipse when wearing approved protective goggles, or view it indirectly with a pinhole camera.

- Be patient when observing the night sky outdoors, as it will take about 20 minutes for your eyes to adjust to the dark. Always dress warmly and use a red filter over a flashlight so that it doesn't affect your night vision.

PROGRESS CHART

Chart your progress as you work through the activity and quiz pages in this book. First check your answers, then color in a star in the correct box below.

Page	Topic	Star	Page	Topic	Star	Page	Topic	Star
14	The Sky at Night	☆	24	The Inner Planets	☆	34	Astronauts	☆
15	Star Distances	☆	25	Our Home Planet	☆	35	Living in Space	☆
16	The Life Cycle of Stars	☆	26	Moon-watching	☆	36	Key Dates of Space Exploration	☆
17	The Milky Way	☆	27	Observing an Eclipse	☆	37	Key Dates of Space Exploration	☆
18	Stargazing	☆	28	The Red Planet	☆	38	Discovering the Universe	☆
19	Stargazing	☆	29	Giant Planets	☆	39	Stars, Galaxies, and Constellations	☆
20	Our Nearest Star	☆	30	Naming the Planets	☆	40	Planets and Smaller Space Bodies	☆
21	Gravity in Space	☆	31	Asteroids, Comets, and Meteors	☆	41	The Sun and Solar System	☆
22	Orbiting the Sun	☆	32	Expanding Universe	☆	42	Earth and the Moon	☆
23	Orbiting the Sun	☆	33	Space Shuttle	☆	43	Astronauts and Spacecraft	☆

Stars and Galaxies

Each tiny star twinkling in the sky is a huge, distant ball of super-hot gas, like our Sun. Each star is part of a group, called a galaxy, that may contain millions of stars. For thousands of years, astronomers gazing at the stars organized them into easily recognizable patterns, called constellations, to create a map of the skies.

Stars

The Milky Way

A star is a huge ball of gas made up mainly of hydrogen. It has a temperature of tens of millions of degrees. The hydrogen fuels nuclear reactions that produce huge amounts of energy. Stars give off most of their energy as light and heat, but they also give off radiation, such as ultraviolet rays and X-rays.

Key facts

- All stars look similar to the naked eye, but in fact they vary in their size, brightness, temperature, and color.
- The stars are hurtling through space at immense speed, but we cannot see this movement because they are so distant.
- Most stars form part of a system containing two or more stars held together by gravity.

Constellations

Astronomers group the brightest stars into constellations. Many constellations are named after characters in ancient mythology, such as Orion and Andromeda. From Earth, the stars in a constellation appear to be close together. In fact, they are great distances apart, but lie in a similar direction from Earth.

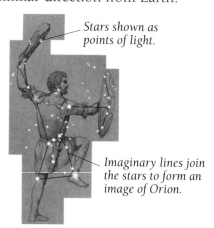

Stars shown as points of light.

Imaginary lines join the stars to form an image of Orion.

The constellation of Orion

Key facts

- Astronomers map the sky by dividing it into 88 areas. Each contains a different constellation.
- Different constellations can be seen from Earth's Northern and Southern Hemispheres.
- Constellations such as Orion that lie along the celestial equator can be seen from both hemispheres.

Galaxies

Every star is part of a vast, spinning group of stars, gas, and dust called a galaxy. The matter in a galaxy is held together by the force of gravity. Galaxies are divided into three main types, according to their shape: spiral, elliptical (oval-shaped), or irregular.

Types of galaxies

Spiral galaxy

Elliptical galaxy

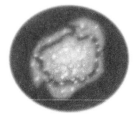

Irregular galaxy

Key facts

- The tiniest dwarf galaxies contain only a few million stars, but giant galaxies can contain hundreds of billions of stars.
- There are about 100 billion galaxies in the part of the Universe that we can observe.
- Our home galaxy, the Milky Way, contains about 200 billion stars.
- Galaxies are grouped together in clusters.

The Solar System

Our nearest star, the Sun, lies along one of the arms of our galaxy, the Milky Way. Earth and seven other planets orbit (move around) the Sun. Smaller bodies, such as moons, asteroids, and comets, orbit the Sun or the planets. All these bodies, together with the Sun, make up the Solar System.

The Sun

The Sun at the center of our Solar System is a relatively small star, known as a yellow dwarf. Like other stars, the Sun's energy is generated by nuclear reactions in its core. The effects of the Sun's light, heat, and radiation can be felt at the farthest edge of the Solar System.

Key facts

- The Sun contains 750 times more matter than all the other bodies in the Solar System put together.
- The Sun's surface is white-hot hydrogen, with a temperature of 9,900°F (5,500°C).
- The Sun's dense core has a temperature of 27 million °F (15 million °C).
- As it is a ball of gas, the Sun does not all rotate at the same speed. Its equator rotates in 25 Earth days, but its poles take 34 days.

Solar System

The Solar System measures about 9,300 billion miles (15,000 billion km) across. The eight planets—Mercury, Venus, Earth, Mars, Jupiter, Saturn, Uranus, and Neptune—occupy only the inner 5.6 billion miles (9 billion km). They travel around the Sun in elliptical (oval) paths known as orbits, trapped by the pull of the Sun's gravity.

Key facts

- All the planets orbit the Sun in the same direction, which is the same direction that the Sun spins on its own axis (the imaginary line from pole to pole).
- The four planets closest to the Sun—Mercury, Venus, Earth, and Mars—are the inner planets.
- The other four planets—Jupiter, Saturn, Uranus, and Neptune—are known as the outer planets.

Asteroids

Asteroids are pieces of rock that orbit the Sun. They measure from about 160 ft (50 m) to 600 miles (1,000 km) across.

Asteroid Ida

Key facts

- Most asteroids are found in the asteroid belt, which lies between the planets Mars and Jupiter.
- Asteroids often collide, breaking into pieces or clumping together to form larger asteroids.

Comets

A comet is a chunk of ice and rock a few miles across that orbits the Sun, often in the far reaches of the Solar System. If a comet nears the Sun it heats up, releasing a glowing tail of dust and gas.

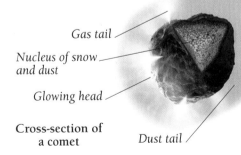

Gas tail

Nucleus of snow and dust

Glowing head

Cross-section of a comet

Dust tail

Key facts

- Comets become visible only as they approach the Sun.
- When Earth passes through the dust from past comets, specks of rock burn up in the atmosphere, producing meteor showers.

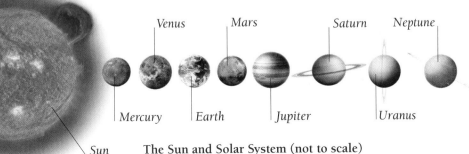

Venus   *Mars*   *Saturn*   *Neptune*

Mercury   *Earth*   *Jupiter*   *Uranus*

Sun   **The Sun and Solar System (not to scale)**

Planets

A planet is a spherical body that orbits the Sun or another star. There are eight planets in our Solar System. These can be divided into two groups: the four rocky planets nearest to the Sun, and the four gas giants beyond the asteroid belt. Most of these planets have bodies orbiting them, known as moons.

Jupiter's moon Callisto

Rocky planets

The four planets nearest to the Sun—Mercury, Venus, Earth, and Mars—are made of rocks and metals. Mercury and Mars have solid iron cores, while the solid cores of Venus and Earth contain iron and nickel. The rocky surfaces of Mercury, Venus, and Mars have many craters. These were formed when the planets were bombarded by rocks from space, called meteorites.

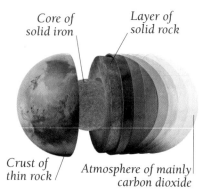

Core of solid iron   Layer of solid rock

Crust of thin rock   Atmosphere of mainly carbon dioxide

Cross-section through Mars

Key facts

- The rocky planets are smaller than the gas planets.
- Earth and Mars are the only rocky planets to have moons.
- The rocky planets have no rings around them.
- Their atmospheres contain very little hydrogen and helium.

Gas planets

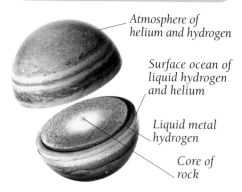

Atmosphere of helium and hydrogen

Surface ocean of liquid hydrogen and helium

Liquid metal hydrogen

Core of rock

Cross-section through Jupiter

Beyond the orbit of Mars lie the four much larger planets— Jupiter, Saturn, Uranus, and Neptune—known as the gas giants. Unlike the rocky planets, these planets do not have solid surfaces. Each has a small, rocky core, surrounded by swirling gases and liquids, and is held together by the force of gravity.

Key facts

- The gas giants have deep, often stormy atmospheres.
- Each gas giant is orbited by a large number of moons.
- A gas giant has a belt of rings, made up of pieces of rock and ice.
- There is high pressure inside the gas giants. This produces more heat from inside these planets than they receive from the Sun.

A moon is a natural object that travels in orbit around a planet. Moons may be the size of a small planet, or just a few miles across. All the planets except Mercury and Venus have moons. Some moons are made from material left over from when their planet formed. Others are asteroids, which have been pulled into a planet's orbit by the force of its gravity.

Saturn's moon Hyperion

Key facts

- Earth's single moon is simply called "the Moon," but other planets' moons have names.
- There are more than 200 known moons in our Solar System.
- Moons are smaller than the planets they orbit.
- Many small moons, such as Hyperion, are not spherical.

Planet Earth

Earth is the only planet we know of where living things exist. It is just near enough to the Sun to give the planet a stable and mild climate, and to allow water to exist in its liquid form. In contrast, our Moon is a barren, airless rock, where no life can survive.

The blue planet

From space, Earth looks like a blue globe, encircled by swirling white clouds. Earth is the only planet with a plentiful supply of water. This not only makes life possible here, but also shapes many of the features of the planet's surface and has a vital role in creating the weather.

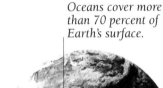
Oceans cover more than 70 percent of Earth's surface.

Earth viewed from space

Key facts

- Earth's atmosphere is made up mainly of nitrogen, oxygen, and carbon dioxide.
- Oxygen in the atmosphere allows humans and animals to breathe.
- Oxygen also forms the ozone layer that protects Earth from radiation from space.
- Carbon dioxide allows plants to survive and create more oxygen.

Earth's orbit

Earth orbits the Sun at a distance of about 93 million miles (150 million km). The time it takes for a planet to orbit the Sun is called its year. Like other planets, Earth also rotates on its axis as it travels. The time it takes a planet to rotate once is its day.

Key facts

- Earth rotates on its axis once every 23 hours 56 minutes. We round this to 24 hours in a day.
- Earth orbits the Sun once every 365.26 days. We round this to 365 days in a normal year.
- The Earth's elliptical (oval) orbit brings it 3 million miles (5 million km) closer to the Sun in January than it is in July.
- Earth orbits the Sun at a speed of 66,000 mph (107,000 kph).

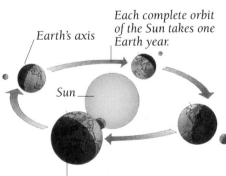
Earth's axis
Each complete orbit of the Sun takes one Earth year.
Sun
Each complete rotation on its axis takes one Earth day.

Earth days and years

The Moon

The Moon orbits Earth, following Earth's journey around the Sun. The Moon does not give off any light of its own, but reflects light from the Sun. As the Moon's position changes relative to the Sun and the Earth, different amounts of moonlight are visible from Earth. The Moon appears to change shape in the sky, starting as a round Full Moon, waning (shrinking) to an invisible New Moon, then waxing (growing) from a crescent to a Full Moon.

The crescent Moon in the night sky

Key facts

- The Moon orbits Earth once every 27.3 days.
- The Moon spins on its axis in exactly the same time that it takes to orbit Earth, so it always has the same side turned towards Earth.
- The Moon takes 29.5 days to go through all its phases (shapes). This is called a lunar month.
- The Moon is more than a quarter the size of Earth, making it the biggest object in the night sky.

The Universe

The Earth is just one small planet in a solar system orbiting a star, which is part of a galaxy of 200 billion stars. That galaxy is just one of tens of billions of galaxies that make up the Universe. The Universe is so large that light from its most distant galaxies takes more than 10 billion years to reach us.

The Big Bang

The Universe explodes into existence in the Big Bang.

Astronomers believe that the Universe began nearly 14 billion years ago with an explosion known as the Big Bang. The Big Bang created an incredibly hot and dense Universe, smaller than an atom. In a fraction of a second, the Universe began to cool and expand in every direction, a process that is still continuing today.

Key facts

- Before the Big Bang, there was nothing: no space, no time, and no matter.
- Scientists do not know what triggered the Big Bang.
- The planets, solar systems, and galaxies are not expanding. It is the space in between the galaxies that is stretching.

How stars form

A star forms from a spinning cloud of gas and dust, called a nebula. The center of the nebula becomes denser and hotter and begins to pull more and more material into itself. Eventually, the center of the nebula becomes so hot and dense that a nuclear reaction takes place, and the star begins to shine.

Key facts

- Galaxies began to form one to two billion years after the Big Bang.
- Our Sun was formed about 4.6 billion years ago.
- Stars are continually being born and dying in the Universe.

Spinning dust and gas

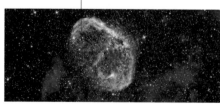

Nebula

Excess material may form planets.

New star

How planets form

As matter spins around a new star, it clumps together to form small bodies called protoplanets. Their gravity pulls in more material, until they form planets.

Material is pulled toward a protoplanet by gravity.

Key facts

- Rocky planets are hot and molten when they first form.
- Gas planets form a solid core, then attract vast amounts of gas.

Evolving Universe

Some scientists believe that the Universe can only expand to a certain size. In billions of years' time, it will shrink and finally collapse. Others believe the Universe will go on expanding forever at the same speed, or at a slower rate.

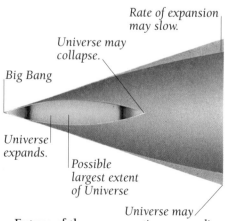

Rate of expansion may slow.

Universe may collapse.

Big Bang

Universe expands.

Possible largest extent of Universe

Future of the Universe

Universe may continue expanding at the same rate.

Looking at Space

Astronomers get most of their information about space by studying pictures and other information from observatories, either on Earth or in orbit around Earth. Scientists have also sent robot probes out into space to visit the planets, asteroids, and comets, giving us close-up views that are impossible to see from Earth.

Observatories

An observatory is a dome that contains a giant telescope. The top of the observatory can turn to face different parts of the sky. Most observatories are located high in the mountains, above the clouds and away from populated areas, where lights make it difficult to get a clear view of the night sky.

Key facts

- Optical telescopes focus light from distant objects and make them clearer.
- Professional astronomers do not actually look through their telescopes. They use them to record images on computers.
- Different types of telescopes can also reveal rays of light that are invisible to human eyes, such as radio waves.

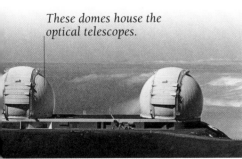

These domes house the optical telescopes.

Mauna Kea Observatory in Hawaii

Space observatories

Space observatories orbit Earth above the atmosphere and give astronomers a clear view of space. Some space observatories, such as the Hubble Space Telescope, are optical telescopes. Others, such as the Chandra X-ray Observatory, view wavelengths that would normally be absorbed by Earth's atmosphere.

Large solar panels power the telescope.

Hubble Space Telescope

Key facts

- A space observatory receives instructions from Earth and transmits images and other data back via an antenna.
- Astronauts aboard the Space Shuttle visited the Hubble Space Telescope five times to install new instruments.
- Space observatories can record gamma rays, X-rays, ultraviolet rays, and infrared rays.

Space probes

A probe is a robot spacecraft sent to investigate space using on-board instruments. The probe flies past or orbits a body in space and sends data and images back to Earth. A probe may also release a lander, to land on the planet, moon, or asteroid beneath it and survey the surface.

Cassini space probe and Saturn

Key facts

- Most space probes are about the size of a family car.
- Space probes are powered by solar panels or a nuclear generator.
- Space probes have given us close-ups of moons, comets, asteroids, and each of the planets.
- After they have completed their missions, some space probes continue out into space, although they can no longer send signals back to Earth.

Galileo space probe

Space Travel

Human space travel began in 1961, when the Russian Yuri Gagarin orbited Earth. US astronauts landed on the Moon eight years later. Today, more than 500 astronauts have traveled into space in rockets or on the space shuttle. In the foreseeable future, astronauts may set up bases on the Moon and may even travel to Mars.

Rockets

A space rocket lifts off from the ground and propels itself into orbit by means of a controlled explosion. Fuel is burned in a combustion chamber to produce a mass of hot gases. The gases expand and explode out of the nozzles at the bottom of the rocket, thrusting it upward.

Key facts

- As the rocket moves away from the pull of Earth's gravity, it can travel much faster.

- Because there is no oxygen in space, a rocket must carry a supply of oxygen to burn its fuel.

- Each section, or stage, of a space rocket fires until its fuel is used up, then falls away.

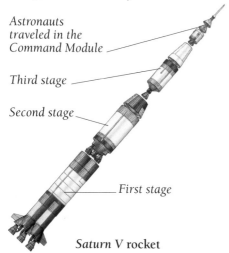

Astronauts traveled in the Command Module

Third stage

Second stage

First stage

Saturn V rocket

Landing craft

Six wheels allow flexibility on bumpy ground.

Camera takes pictures of the area ahead.

Mars rover

A manned or unmanned vehicle can land on a planet, moon, or asteroid, collect samples, take photographs, and carry out experiments. The landing craft has to be designed to function in difficult surface conditions, such as extreme temperatures or very low gravity. A rover vehicle has wheels so that it can survey a wider area.

Key facts

- Mars is the only planet that has been visited by robot vehicles. The rovers found frozen water in the Martian rocks.

- The Moon is the only body that humans have landed on.

- On three of the six Apollo missions that landed on the Moon, astronauts used a vehicle called a lunar rover to travel around.

Space shuttle

The space shuttle was the first reusable spacecraft. It was made up of a winged orbiter that carried the crew and the cargo, twin booster rockets, and a fuel tank. It took off like a rocket, but landed like an aircraft. The first space shuttle, *Columbia*, was launched in 1981. The last space shuttle mission was by *Atlantis* in 2011.

Space shuttle on takeoff

Key facts

- The space shuttle was used to launch space probes and satellites, and to carry out repairs and construction work in space.

- There were five space shuttle orbiters, but two were destroyed in accidents.

- The external fuel tank was the only part that could not be reused.

Silica tiles protect the shuttle from burning up as it reenters Earth's atmosphere.

Space shuttle landing

Living in Space

Only 24 astronauts have traveled beyond Earth's orbit as far as the Moon. Most astronauts orbit Earth in their spacecraft, or travel to space stations. Their mission may be to release a satellite into orbit, to carry out maintenance to a space station or an observatory, or to conduct experiments into conditions in space.

Astronauts

Astronaut spacewalking

A person travelling in space is called an astronaut, or cosmonaut if he or she is part of a Russian mission. Astronauts train for over a year before making their first space flight. Most are experts in one or more sciences, so they can carry out scientific research while they are in space.

Key facts

- Astronauts have to be extremely fit to withstand conditions in space.
- A spacesuit is worn outside the spacecraft to protect the astronaut from temperature extremes and to provide oxygen.
- Spacewalking astronauts are attached to the craft by tethers so that they do not float away.

Space stations

A space station is a spacecraft designed to stay in orbit for many years. On board, astronauts conduct experiments to discover how conditions in space affect people, plants, and animals. Astronauts may stay on board a space station for over a year. Spacecraft make regular visits to bring supplies and change the crews of astronauts.

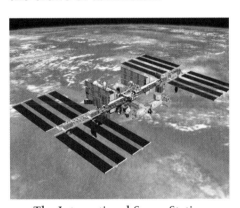

The International Space Station

Key facts

- Space stations are carried into space in sections and put together by astronauts.
- The first space station, *Salyut 1*, was launched in 1971.
- At nearly 360 ft (100 m) long, the International Space Station is the biggest structure ever built in space.

Life on board

In space there is no feeling of gravity, so everything becomes almost weightless. Astronauts and their equipment float around inside spacecraft unless they are strapped down. Lack of gravity means that the body does not have to work so hard, so astronauts have to exercise to keep muscles from wasting away. They monitor their bodies constantly to check their health and study the effects of space travel on the human body.

Astronaut in zero gravity

Key facts

- In future, food may be grown in space, but at present all food and water have to be brought to the space station from Earth.
- Life support systems provide oxygen and filter out the carbon dioxide that people breathe out.
- Astronauts sleep strapped into bags that hold them in place so that they do not float around inside the spacecraft.

Sleeping equipment

The Sky at Night

The best time to observe the stars is on a dark, clear night. You will see more in the countryside, away from the hazy glow of city lights. Binoculars or a telescope will help you observe distant objects more clearly, but even with the naked eye you can still see constellations, bright stars and planets, and the Moon.

It takes several minutes for your eyes to get used to darkness. Then, fainter objects in the sky will become visible.

Watching the night sky

These pictures show some things that you can see in the night sky. Read each caption, then write the letter of the picture it describes in the box.

a

b

c

d

1. With binoculars, you can see craters on the surface of the Moon.

2. The Milky Way looks like a band of dust sprinkled across the sky.

3. Nicknamed the evening star, the planet Venus can often be seen in the early evening, or just after dawn.

4. On a clear night, you may see a shooting star every 15 minutes or so. It looks like a long streak of light.

How a telescope works

Look carefully at this diagram of a reflecting telescope, then fill in the missing words to complete the facts. Choose from:

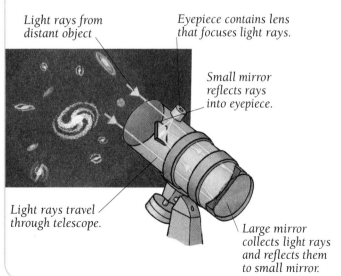

Light rays from distant object

Eyepiece contains lens that focuses light rays.

Small mirror reflects rays into eyepiece.

Light rays travel through telescope.

Large mirror collects light rays and reflects them to small mirror.

mirrors   lens   reflects   light rays   eyepiece

1. Most astronomical telescopes are reflecting telescopes, which use..to reflect light.

2. A large, curved mirror at the bottom of the tube gathers...from distant objects and reflects them back up the body of the telescope.

3. A smaller, flat mirror...........................the light rays onto an eyepiece at the side of the tube.

4. The image that the astronomer sees through the ....is upside down.

5. A small..in the eyepiece magnifies the image.

Star Distances

The stars lie so far away from Earth that astronomers cannot measure the distance in miles. They measure distances in light years. One light year is how far light travels in one year—a distance of 5,900 billion miles (9,500 billion km). Light travels at more than 670 million mph (1 billion kph).

Vast distances

The stars in a constellation like Cassiopeia are great distances apart. However, they look close together when viewed from Earth.

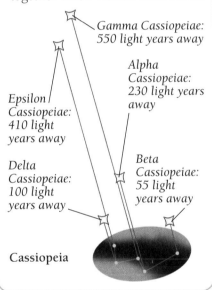

Gamma Cassiopeiae: 550 light years away

Alpha Cassiopeiae: 230 light years away

Epsilon Cassiopeiae: 410 light years away

Delta Cassiopeiae: 100 light years away

Beta Cassiopeiae: 55 light years away

Cassiopeia

Light years away

Draw a line to match each star's distance from Earth in light years to its distance in miles. Start by figuring out which is the biggest distance in light years and match it to the biggest distance in miles, and so on.

Star	Distance in light years	Distance
1. Sirius A	8.6	1,829,000 billion miles (2,945,000 billion km)
2. Canopus	310	149,270 billion miles (240,350 billion km)
3. Arcturus	36.8	50,740 billion miles (81,700 billion km)
4. Vega	25.3	217,120 billion miles (349,600 billion km)

Star colors

The color of a star shows the temperature of its surface. Astronomers divide stars into seven types, depending on their temperature. Use the star type table to answer the questions below.

Type	Color		Average temperature
O	Blue	●	80,000°F (45,000°C)
B	Bluish-white	●	55,000°F (30,000°C)
A	White	○	22,000°F (12,000°C)
F	Yellowish-white		14,000°F (8,000°C)
G	Yellow	●	12,000°F (6,500°C)
K	Orange	●	9,000°F (5,000°C)
M	Red	●	6,500°F (3,500°C)

1. Which type of star is hottest? ....

2. Which color are type G stars, like our Sun?......................................

3. What is the average temperature of orange stars?................................

4. Which four types of stars are hotter than our Sun?....................

The Life Cycle of Stars

Our Sun's life will last about 10 billion years. When it runs out of fuel, the Sun will expand to form a red giant. Bigger stars live only a few million years before they swell into supergiants. Stars that are smaller than our Sun may live 100 billion years.

Life and death of a star

Color in the red supergiant, red giant, and black dwarf to complete this diagram.

A **nebula** is a great cloud of dust and hydrogen gas. New stars are born in the nebula.

A **star** begins to shine when nuclear reactions inside the core produce heat and light.

When a massive star, hundreds of times bigger than our Sun, begins to run out of fuel, it cools down, glows red, and begins to swell into a **red supergiant**.

The core of a supernova may collapse and become a very dense **neutron star** that continues to spin through space.

The core of a supernova may collapse to form a **black hole**, an area of space with such powerful gravity that it sucks in everything, even light.

The core of the supergiant eventually blasts apart in an explosion called a **supernova**. It can be as bright as a whole galaxy.

When a smaller star, like our Sun, runs low on fuel, it expands into a **red giant**. It glows red as it cools.

The outer layers of gas puff out like a ring of smoke to form a **planetary nebula**.

The faint, shrunken remains of the star become a **white dwarf**. They glow white as they cool.

When the star is so cool that it has stopped glowing, it forms a **black dwarf**.

Star knowledge

Complete the sentences by circling the right answers. Use the information on this page to help you.

1. Our Sun will live for about **5 / 10 / 15** billion years.

2. When the Sun eventually starts to cool down, it will expand and become a **red giant / red supergiant / neutron star**.

3. A black dwarf is a star that **is being formed / is shining / has stopped glowing**.

4. Black holes are formed when **supernovas / small stars / nebulas** collapse.

The Milky Way

We call the cloud of light that arches across the night sky the Milky Way. In fact, this hazy band of stars and dust is only part of our home galaxy. Almost everything we can see in the night sky is part of the Milky Way.

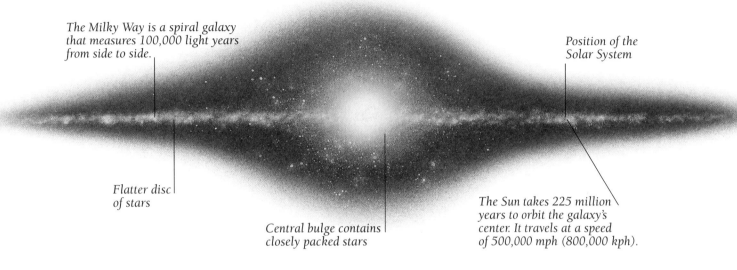

The Milky Way is a spiral galaxy that measures 100,000 light years from side to side.

Position of the Solar System

Flatter disc of stars

Central bulge contains closely packed stars

The Sun takes 225 million years to orbit the galaxy's center. It travels at a speed of 500,000 mph (800,000 kph).

The Milky Way in numbers

Draw a line to match each item to the right number. You will find information to help you above and on page 6.

1. The width of the Milky Way, in light years   **100 billion**

2. The number of galaxies in the part of the Universe we can observe   **100,000**

3. The number of years the Sun takes to orbit the center of the Milky Way   **200 billion**

4. The speed at which the Sun travels around the galaxy   **225 million**

5. The number of stars in the Milky Way   **500,000 mph (800,000 kph)**

Spot the galaxy

Look closely at these photos of galaxies. Can you identify the three different types using the information on page 6? Draw a line to link each label to the right picture.

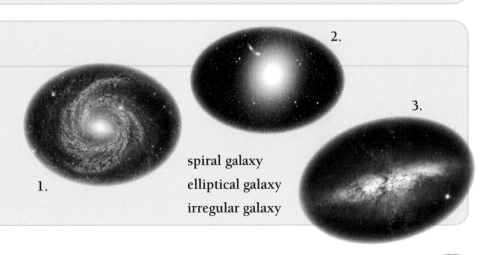

spiral galaxy

elliptical galaxy

irregular galaxy

Stargazing

Many of the constellations, or patterns of stars, that we observe today were first picked out and named by ancient Greek and Roman stargazers. More recently, in the 15th and 16th centuries, European seafarers saw the Southern Hemisphere's stars for the first time, and invented new constellations.

Northern polar stars

This map shows the stars that can be seen in the Northern Hemisphere. The red lines show the area that forms each constellation. Match each constellation on the polar map to a picture around the page by writing its letter in the correct box.

2. This constellation represents **Cepheus**, the husband of Cassiopeia below. Joining together some of its stars makes a shape like a child's drawing of a house.

1. The brightest star in **Ursa Minor**, the Little Bear, is Polaris, the Pole Star. The star is used by navigators to find north.

3. Within **Ursa Major**, the Great Bear, seven bright stars form a pattern called the Big Dipper, which can be seen with the naked eye.

4. The ancient Greeks named this large, W-shaped constellation after the vain queen **Cassiopeia**. They pictured her admiring herself in a mirror.

5. The large constellation of **Draco**, the Dragon, wraps around the body of Ursa Minor.

Southern polar stars

This map shows the stars that can be seen in the Southern Hemisphere. The red lines show the area that forms each constellation. Match each constellation on the polar map to a picture around the page by writing its letter in the correct box.

1. Several constellations make up a boat shape. **Carina**, the Keel, is its bottom.

2. Hydrus, the Little Water Snake, forms a zigzag in the sky.

3. The **Southern Cross** is the smallest constellation in the sky, but its four prominent stars make it easily recognizable.

4. Centaurus represents a mythical beast called a centaur, which was half-man and half-horse.

5. Triangulum Australe, the Southern Triangle, lies beneath the front hooves of Centaurus.

Did you know?

A constellation named after a mythical being often lies close to characters from the same story. Cassiopeia, for example, is near her husband, Cepheus; her daughter, Andromeda; and the hero Perseus, who rescued Andromeda from a sea monster.

Our Nearest Star

The Sun is a giant ball of glowing gases, 100 times wider than Earth. Its surface layer, the photosphere, is 60 miles (100 km) deep. The photosphere is a bubbling mass of hot gases, like a stormy sea of fire. Constant explosions send up jets of hot, burning gas.

> **WARNING** Never look directly at the Sun. Its glare could blind you.

Sun facts

- All the Sun's energy is produced in its core. The energy gradually radiates (moves) outward until it reaches the Sun's surface.
- Sunspots are darker patches on the Sun's surface. Their temperature is about 2,700°F (1,500°C) cooler than the rest of the surface.
- The pearl-white atmosphere around the Sun is called the corona. Its temperature can reach 5.4 million °F (3 million °C).
- The Sun sends fountains of glowing gas, called prominences, into the corona. The prominences may be up to 37,000 miles (60,000 km) high.

Parts of the Sun

Can you name the different parts of the Sun? Draw a line to link each label to the right part of the picture using the information on this page to help you.

sunspot

corona

prominence

core

photosphere

True or false?

Read the following statements about the Sun. Use the information on this page and page 7 to figure out which statements are true and which are false, then check the right boxes.

	TRUE	FALSE
1. The Sun is the star at the center of our Solar System.	☐	☐
2. The Sun orbits the Earth and other planets.	☐	☐
3. The Sun is a giant ball of oxygen gas.	☐	☐
4. Sunspots are the hottest regions on the Sun's surface.	☐	☐
5. The outer atmosphere of the Sun is called the corona.	☐	☐

Gravity in Space

Every object in the Universe has its own pulling force called gravity. Gravity keeps the Solar System's planets in orbit around the Sun, and the Milky Way spinning in space. The greater an object's mass (the more matter it contains), the greater its gravity.

Gravity facts

- Earth has more mass than the Moon, so its gravity keeps the Moon in orbit around it.
- On Earth, gravity pulls us toward the planet's center, keeping our feet on the ground.
- On the Moon, you would weigh only one-sixth of your weight on Earth.
- The Moon's gravity raises tides on Earth, causing the oceans to rise and fall each day.
- Astronauts in orbit do not feel the pull of Earth's gravity, so they float around in their spacecraft.
- In order to escape the pull of Earth's gravity, rockets must reach a speed of over 25,000 mph (40,000 kph). This is known as escape velocity.

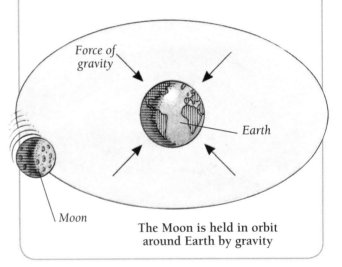

Force of gravity

Earth

Moon

The Moon is held in orbit around Earth by gravity

Orbiting objects

Use information on this page to figure out whether any of the things in the list orbit the Moon, Earth, or Sun. Write the names of the correct orbiting objects under each picture. Choose from:

planets   Moon   Earth   space station   satellite

MOON
....
....
....

EARTH
....
....
....

SUN
....
....
....

Birth of the Solar System

Read the captions carefully and then number them 1 to 4 to show how the Solar System began. Use the information on page 10 to help you.

a. Fragments of matter are attracted to each other by gravity. They clump together to form objects called protoplanets.

Sun

Rocky planets forming in inner Solar System

Gas planets forming in outer Solar System

b. The gravity of protoplanets near the Solar System's center pulls in rock, and the rocky planets form. The gravity of the outer protoplanets attracts gas, and the gas planets form.

c. A spinning disc forms around the Sun, made of matter blown off during its birth.

d. A cloud of spinning dust and gas called a nebula collapses to form the Sun.

Orbiting the Sun

The eight planets of our Solar System orbit or travel around the Sun at different distances, and take different lengths of time to complete one orbit. The amount of time a planet takes to orbit the Sun is called its orbital period or year. The time a planet takes to rotate on its axis once is called its rotation period or day.

Planets of the Solar System

Fill in the name of each planet on this Solar System diagram by comparing the facts here with those on the chart on page 47.

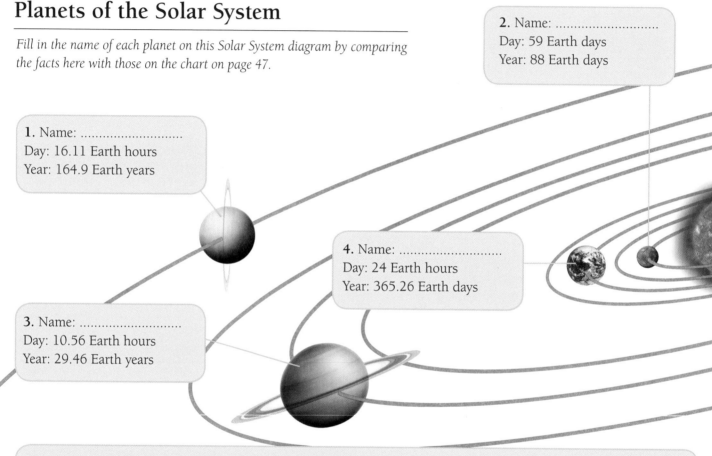

2. Name: ....
Day: 59 Earth days
Year: 88 Earth days

1. Name: ....
Day: 16.11 Earth hours
Year: 164.9 Earth years

4. Name: ....
Day: 24 Earth hours
Year: 365.26 Earth days

3. Name: ....
Day: 10.56 Earth hours
Year: 29.46 Earth years

Planet puzzles

Complete the sentences by circling the right words. Use the information on this page to help you.

1. The planet with the longest year is **Earth / Mercury / Neptune**.

2. A year on Uranus lasts **84 Earth years / 84 Earth days / 11.86 Earth days**.

3. A day on Mercury lasts **59 Earth days / 59 Earth hours / 5.9 Earth hours**.

4. Two planets have shorter years than Earth. They are **Uranus and Neptune / Mercury and Venus / Jupiter and Saturn**.

Earth time teasers

It takes one day for the Earth to spin around once on its axis.
It takes one year for the Earth to orbit the Sun.

1 day = 1 spin
1 year = 1 orbit

1. How many spins are there in a week?

⬚ spins

2. How many orbits are there in a century?

⬚ orbits

3. How many spins are there until your next birthday?

⬚ spins

4. How many orbits and spins old is your best friend?

⬚ ⬚
orbits spins

5. Name: ....
Day: 17.24 Earth hours
Year: 84 Earth years

6. Name: ....
Day: 243 Earth days
Year: 224.7 Earth days

7. Name: ....
Day: 9.93 Earth hours
Year: 11.86 Earth years

8. Name: ....
Day: 24.63 Earth hours
Year: 687 Earth days

Did you know?

As they orbit the Sun, planets nearer to the center of the Solar System travel through space faster than planets farther away.

Seeing the Solar System to scale

The diagram of the Solar System on this page is not drawn to scale because this book is not wide enough to show you the Solar System's vast scale. Try making a diagram that gives you an idea of how far each planet is from the Sun.

1 Draw pictures of each planet and the Sun. Color them in and cut them out.

2 Find a long strip of wallpaper or other paper, about 15 ft (5 m) long. Stick the Sun at one end of the paper.

3 Measure the following distances from the Sun to stick down the eight planets:

Mercury: 2½ in (6 cm)   Jupiter: 2 ft 7 in (78 cm)
Venus: 4½ in (11 cm)   Saturn: 4 ft 7 in (1.4 m)
Earth: 6 in (15 cm)   Uranus: 9 ft 6 in (2.9 m)
Mars: 9 in (23 cm)   Neptune: 14 ft 9 in (4.5 m)

4 Look on the Solar System fact chart to find out how far each planet is from the Sun. Label each planet with its name and distance.

The Inner Planets

Mercury, the closest planet to the Sun, has almost no atmosphere to protect it from the Sun or to trap heat. Temperatures soar in the day, then plummet at night. Mercury's neighbor, Venus, is the Solar System's hottest planet, because its cloudy atmosphere traps heat.

Venus

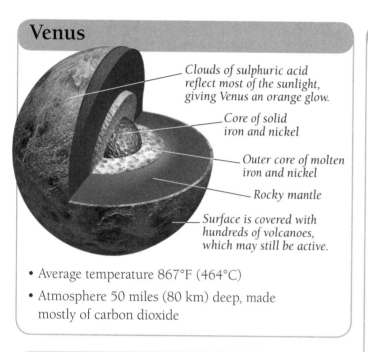

Clouds of sulphuric acid reflect most of the sunlight, giving Venus an orange glow.

Core of solid iron and nickel

Outer core of molten iron and nickel

Rocky mantle

Surface is covered with hundreds of volcanoes, which may still be active.

- Average temperature 867°F (464°C)
- Atmosphere 50 miles (80 km) deep, made mostly of carbon dioxide

Mercury

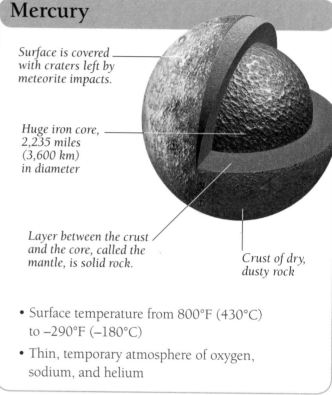

Surface is covered with craters left by meteorite impacts.

Huge iron core, 2,235 miles (3,600 km) in diameter

Layer between the crust and the core, called the mantle, is solid rock.

Crust of dry, dusty rock

- Surface temperature from 800°F (430°C) to −290°F (−180°C)
- Thin, temporary atmosphere of oxygen, sodium, and helium

Venus time teasers

Venus spins very slowly on its axis, so on Venus a day is longer than a year.

    1 Venus day = 243 Earth days
    1 Venus year = 224.7 Earth days

Figure out how old you are in Venus time. You will need a calculator for this.

1 Multiply your age in years by 365 to figure out your age in Earth days.
Age in Earth years:..
Age in Earth days:..

2 Divide your answer by 243 to find out how many Venus days old you are.
Age in Venus days:..

3 Divide your age in Earth days by 224.7 to find out how old you are in Venus years.
Age in Venus years:..

Mercury or Venus?

Check whether the answer to each of the questions below is Mercury or Venus. Use information on this page and the fact chart on page 47 to help you.

	Mercury	Venus
1. Which planet is hotter?	☐	☐
2. Which planet is closer to the Sun?	☐	☐
3. Which planet has a longer day?	☐	☐
4. Which planet has a thicker atmosphere?	☐	☐
5. Which planet is bigger?	☐	☐

Our Home Planet

Earth is the third planet from the Sun, and the largest rocky planet. Its atmosphere extends more than 375 miles (600 km) into space. The atmosphere circulates heat from the warm Equator to the freezing poles, giving Earth an average temperature of 59°F (15°C).

Earth from space

Read the captions below about planet Earth, then draw a line to link each caption to the right part of the picture.

1. Land areas that appear yellow-brown from space are mainly deserts.

2. Land areas that appear green are forests and grasslands.

3. Oceans cover more than 70 percent of Earth's surface.

4. Icecaps at the poles contain just 2 percent of Earth's water.

5. Clouds of water vapor swirl around the atmosphere.

Inside Earth facts

Upper mantle of partly molten rock

Thick mantle of heavy rock

Outer core of molten iron

Inner core of hot, dense solid iron

Rocky crust is thinner beneath the sea than under landmasses.

Earth challenge

Fill in the missing words to complete these sentences. Use the information on this page and on the fact chart on page 47 to help you. Choose from:

atmosphere   iron   landmasses   icecaps   Sun

1. Earth's core is made of..

2. Earth is 92.9 million miles (149.6 million km) from the..

3. The..stretches more than 375 miles (600 km) above Earth's surface.

4. Two percent of the water on Earth is trapped in its polar..

5. Earth's crust is thickest under................................

Moon-watching

It is easy to study the changing shapes, or phases, of the Moon with your eyes alone. But if you have a pair of binoculars, you will also be able to see details of the Moon's surface, such as craters and mountains.

Phases of the Moon

- When the Moon is directly between the Sun and the Earth, the side facing us is dark. We call it a New Moon.
- As the Moon continues on its orbit of Earth, it appears to grow bigger (wax) as more of it is lit up.
- We see the entire face of the Moon at Full Moon.
- After the Full Moon, the Moon appears to shrink (wane) until it disappears again.

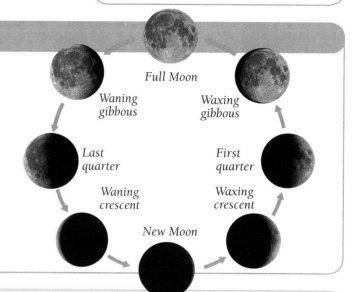

Moon log

Look at the phases of the Moon above. Try keeping your own record of how the Moon's shape changes over the course of a month.

1. After dark, look for the Moon in the night sky.

2. Use a black pen to color in part of the first circle to show the Moon's shape.

3. Write the date underneath your entry.

4. Repeat every day for four weeks, until the chart is full.

5. If you forget one evening, or if the Moon is hidden by clouds, put an x through that night's circle.

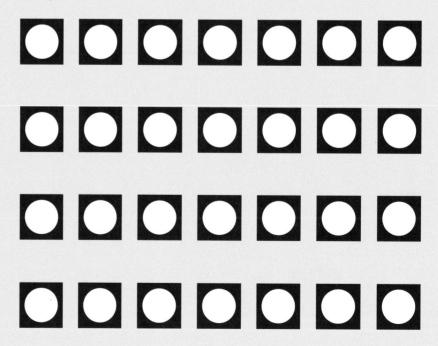

Observing an Eclipse

As the Moon orbits Earth, it sometimes moves in front of the Sun, casting a shadow on Earth and blocking out the Sun. This eerie phenomenon, when daylight disappears, is called a solar eclipse.

How a solar eclipse works

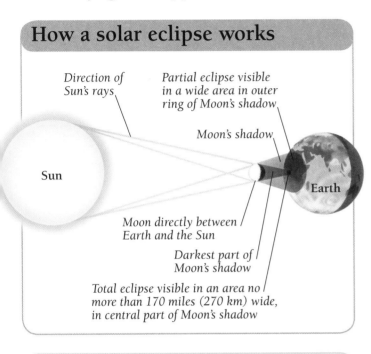

Direction of Sun's rays

Partial eclipse visible in a wide area in outer ring of Moon's shadow

Moon's shadow

Sun

Earth

Moon directly between Earth and the Sun

Darkest part of Moon's shadow

Total eclipse visible in an area no more than 170 miles (270 km) wide, in central part of Moon's shadow

Eclipse in action

These pictures show the stages of a solar eclipse viewed from Earth. Number the captions in the right order to follow the sequence from top to bottom.

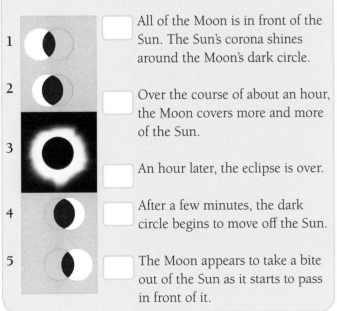

1
2
3
4
5

☐ All of the Moon is in front of the Sun. The Sun's corona shines around the Moon's dark circle.

☐ Over the course of about an hour, the Moon covers more and more of the Sun.

☐ An hour later, the eclipse is over.

☐ After a few minutes, the dark circle begins to move off the Sun.

☐ The Moon appears to take a bite out of the Sun as it starts to pass in front of it.

Lunar eclipse

Try this experiment to find out why the Moon glows red in a lunar eclipse. You need a dark room, a desk lamp, a globe, a ball, and a clear bottle containing water and one teaspoon of milk.

1 Line up the globe and the lamp.

2 Switch on the lamp and place the ball in the globe's shadow. The ball will be completely dark.

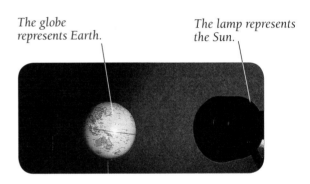

The globe represents Earth.

The lamp represents the Sun.

3 Hold the bottle on top of the globe and watch the ball. The milky water scatters the light, just like Earth's atmosphere, casting a pink glow on the ball.

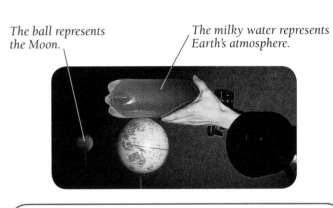

The ball represents the Moon.

The milky water represents Earth's atmosphere.

WARNING Never look directly at a solar eclipse and never view it using a telescope, binoculars, or a mirror. View it indirectly with a pinhole camera or observe it through approved protective goggles.

The Red Planet

In the night sky, the distinctive orange-red color of Mars is easy to see with the naked eye. Mars is the outermost of the four rocky planets, and only about half the size of Earth. Today, its surface is a bitterly cold desert, but three billion years ago, Mars was much warmer and water flowed there.

> **Did you know?**
>
> Olympus Mons on Mars is the largest volcano in the Solar System. It stands about 15 miles (24 km) high. That is nearly three times as tall as the highest mountain on Earth, Mount Everest.

Mars in close-up

Figure out which part of the picture each caption refers to, then write the correct letter in the box.

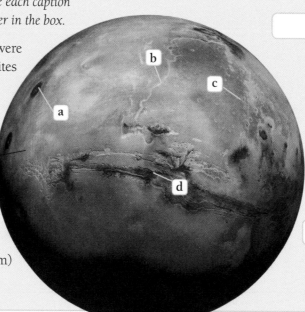

1. Lots of small craters were formed when meteorites bombarded Mars 4 billion years ago.

Red color is caused by iron oxide (rust) in the rocks and soil.

2. The long slit across Mars is the Valles Marineris, a 2,800-mile (4,500-km) system of canyons.

3. The Kasei Vallis is a curved canyon north of the Valles Marineris. It was created by heavy flooding when Mars had a plentiful supply of water.

4. Dark circles on the surface of Mars are giant extinct volcanoes.

Make some Martian dust

To make some Martian dust, you will need some sand, a tray, rubber gloves, scissors, steel wool, and water.

1 Half-fill the tray with sand. Wearing gloves, cut the steel wool into pieces and mix it into the sand. Wet the sand. Leave the tray uncovered in a safe place.

2 Check the sand every day, and add more water if it dries out. How long does it take for the sand to turn a rusty red color?

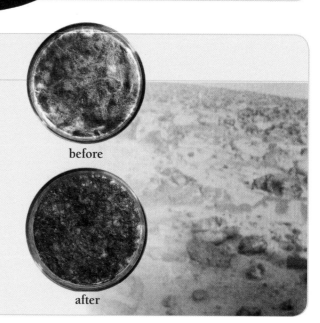

before

after

Giant Planets

The gas planets—Jupiter, Saturn, Uranus, and Neptune—are much bigger than the rocky inner planets. Unlike the rocky planets, the gas planets have no solid surface, just a swirling layer of gas and liquid.

Which planet?

Read these planet facts. Then color in each planet according to its description. Use pages 22 and 23 to help you.

Jupiter

- Jupiter is so large that more than 1,300 Earths would fit inside it.
- Jupiter's Great Red Spot is a giant storm, three times as large as Earth.
- Chemicals such as sulphur and ammonia form colored bands across the atmosphere.
- Jupiter has a faint system of three thin rings.

Uranus

- Uranus has a greenish-blue atmosphere with no cloud bands or storms.
- The axis of Uranus is so tilted that the planet moves along its orbital path on its side.
- Uranus has 11 rings, which are at almost 90 degrees to the planet's orbit.

Saturn

- Saturn is the most distant planet that can be seen from Earth with the naked eye.
- Saturn's system of seven shining rings is more than twice the diameter of the planet itself and can be seen from Earth with a telescope.
- Saturn's yellow color is made by clouds of ammonia in its atmosphere.

Neptune

- Neptune has a deep blue atmosphere, often streaked with bands of white cloud.
- Heat from within Neptune's core creates fast winds and colossal storms. The storms look like dark spots on the planet's surface.
- Neptune has five thin complete rings and one partial ring.

Gas planet puzzle

Complete these statements about the gas planets by circling the right words. Use the information on this page to help you.

1. Jupiter's giant storm is called the **Great Red Spot / Great Yellow Spot / Great Dark Spot**.

2. **Neptune / Uranus / Saturn** moves sideways along its orbit.

3. The surface of gas planets is made of **molten metal / gas and liquid / jagged rocks**.

4. The planet with the most rings is **Jupiter / Saturn / Uranus**.

Naming the Planets

The Romans named the five planets they could see after their gods. Today, we still use the same names. Uranus and Neptune were discovered later, after the invention of the telescope, but they, too, were given the names of Roman gods.

Planet names puzzle

Read the description beneath each god, then write in the name. Use the charts on pages 47 and 48 and information on page 7 to help you. Choose from:

**Mercury   Venus   Mars   Jupiter
Saturn   Uranus   Neptune**

1. ....
The largest planet is named after the king of the gods.

2. ....
The blood-red planet nearest to Earth is named after the god of war.

5. ....
The Romans named the most distant planet that they could see after the father of the gods.

3. ....
The planet that orbits the Sun at the fastest speed is named after the swift messenger of the gods.

4. ....
The farthest planet from the Sun was named after the god of the sea, because it looks blue.

6. ....
When a planet beyond Saturn was discovered in 1781, it was named after the father of Saturn.

7. ....
The hottest planet glows so brightly that it was named after the goddess of beauty.

Planet challenge

Answer these questions about the planets. Use the charts on pages 47 and 48 for help.

1. Which planet is the biggest?

....

2. Which two planets have no moons?

....

3. Which planet is farthest from the Sun?

....

4. Which planet has the largest rings?

....

5. Which is the windiest planet?

....

Asteroids, Comets, and Meteors

Between the planets and moons, smaller objects such as asteroids and meteors move around the Solar System. These objects are made from material left over from the formation of the Solar System. Even smaller, icier objects are found beyond Neptune, in the Kuiper Belt. Some of these become comets heading toward the Sun.

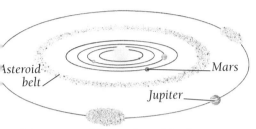

Most **asteroids** are found in the 112 million-mile (180 million-km) wide asteroid belt that lies between Mars and Jupiter.

Halley's Comet returns to the inner Solar System once every 76 years. The first recorded sighting was by Chinese astronomers in 240 BCE.

In 2006, astronomers decided that **Pluto**, which had been discovered in 1930, is too small to be a planet. It is now classed as a dwarf planet.

Meteors are lumps of space rock or metal. We see them as **shooting stars** if they burn up in the atmosphere.

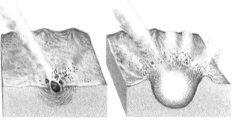

If a meteor is too large to burn up in the atmosphere, and hits the Earth, its impact may form a **crater**.

Most meteors burn up. Those that reach the ground—about 3,000 each year—are called **meteorites**.

Small space bodies

Complete these facts by circling the right answers. Use information from this page to help you.

1. Since 2006, Pluto has been classed as a **planet / star / dwarf planet**.

2. Rocks that hit Earth and other planets are called **craters / meteorites / asteroids**.

3. Shooting stars are **comets / meteors / stars** falling through the atmosphere.

4. Halley's **Star / Comet / Meteor** returns to the inner Solar System once every 76 years.

5. Most asteroids are found in the **Kuiper Belt / asteroid belt / astral belt** between Mars and Jupiter.

6. Craters are formed when big **stars / meteorites / moons** hit Earth.

Expanding Universe

The Universe has not always existed. It began nearly 14 billion years ago when the Big Bang created time and matter. Astronomers know that the Universe is still expanding because almost all of the galaxies they can see are moving apart.

After the Big Bang

Read the captions to find out the order in which the Universe began. Then fill in the gaps using the words from the list below.

Solar System	galaxies	atoms
Big Bang	Milky Way	

14 billion years ago, the Universe began with the ....

13 billion years ago, the first .... began to form.

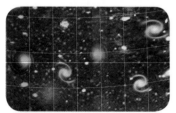

12 billion years ago, matter clumped together to form the first ....

11 billion years ago, the oldest stars in the .... were born.

4.6 billion years ago, our .... was formed.

Expansion facts

- The galaxies are not expanding, but the space between them is.
- Three billion years ago, clusters of galaxies were 25 percent nearer to each other than they are today.

| *Three billion years ago* | *The present* | *Two billion years in the future* |

- Two billion years in the future, the clusters will be 15 percent farther apart.

Watch the Universe expand

Read the facts above to see how the Universe is expanding. Try this activity to see how this expansion is possible.

1 Half blow up a balloon, then hold the end shut. The balloon represents the Universe.

2 Draw dots on the balloon in marker, two finger-widths apart. The dots represent galaxies.

3 Finish blowing up the balloon. Tie the end.

4 Look at the spaces between the dots now. How many finger-widths apart are they?

finger-widths

Space Shuttle

Before the invention of the space shuttle, spacecraft were used only once. Astronauts returned to Earth by splashing down into the ocean inside a section of the spacecraft, or by parachuting from the spacecraft before it crash-landed. The space shuttle, however, landed like a plane with the astronauts on board. The last space shuttle mission was in 2011, 30 years after the first.

Into orbit and back again

Read the captions below and look at the pictures. Number them 1 to 6 to show what happened on a space shuttle mission.

Protective silica tiles glowed as the orbiter reentered the atmosphere.

The orbiter's main engines and rocket boosters fired together at liftoff.

Eight minutes after takeoff, the external fuel tank dropped away.

The orbiter remained in orbit for up to two weeks.

The orbiter glided in to land on an ordinary runway.

Two minutes after liftoff, the rocket boosters fell back to Earth.

Parts of the orbiter

Read the captions below about the space shuttle orbiter. Draw a line to link each one to the correct part of the picture.

The **payload bay** carried the payload (cargo) such as satellites or space station parts.

The **mechanical arm** moved objects in and out of the payload bay.

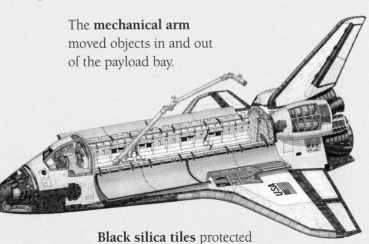

The **payload bay doors** were opened in orbit to prevent the orbiter from overheating.

The **cabin** housed the crew. It contained the flight deck and bunks. An airlock gave access to space.

Black silica tiles protected the craft from burning as it reentered the atmosphere.

The **wings** had no function in space but helped the orbiter glide when it landed.

Astronauts

An astronaut's spacesuit carries essential supplies. It has oxygen for breathing, water for maintaining a comfortable body temperature, and electrical power. Today's spacesuits are so advanced that astronauts can safely and easily move around outside their spacecraft and carry out delicate repairs to equipment out in space.

Did you know?

The oldest person ever to go into space was US astronaut John Glenn. When he traveled aboard the space shuttle in 1998, he was 77 years old.

Astronaut suit

Read these captions about astronauts' spacesuits. Looking at the pictures for clues, fill in the missing words. Choose from:

gloves   visor   outersuit   helmet   undersuit   boots

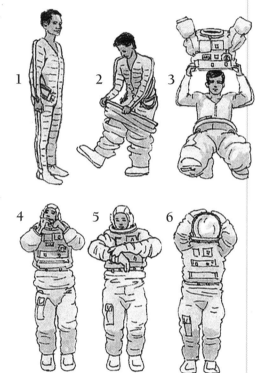

1. The astronaut's.................................has a network of water-filled tubing. This helps the body stay at the right temperature.

2. The...........................attach to the legs of the suit. There are tight seams and seals between the different parts of the suit to stop any oxygen leaks.

3. The.................................... contains a synthetic fiber called Kevlar, which can withstand high temperatures and is also used for bulletproof vests.

4. A cap inside the...........................contains communications equipment.

5. The astronaut's.............................contain their own heating units. These keep the hands warm but are flexible to allow movement.

6. The helmet's mirrored........................... protects the astronaut from the Sun's glare.

Astronauts at work

Circle the right words to complete these sentences. Use information on this page and page 13.

1. Most astronauts are experts in **geography / history / science**.

2. Spacecraft carry space stations into space in sections, which are put together by **astronauts / aliens / builders**.

3. Outside the spacecraft, an astronaut carries a supply of **food / oxygen / carbon dioxide** so he or she can breathe.

4. Astronauts from Russia are called **russianauts / marinauts / cosmonauts**.

Living in Space

In space, everything is almost weightless. People, equipment, and even food float around inside a spacecraft if they are not strapped down or contained. Astronauts prepare for life in space by training in water tanks. The experience of being under water is similar to the weightlessness in space.

Did you know?

There is no floor or ceiling in an orbiting spacecraft. That is because there is no feeling of gravity in space, so there is no such thing as up or down!

Gravity facts

- Liquids and crumbs of food would float away in a spacecraft. Food has to be kept in sealed containers.
- Dust does not settle in a spacecraft. It has to be vacuumed out of the air.
- On Earth, gravity pulls the ink in a pen down toward the nib. In space, pens have to have a special mechanism that pushes the ink toward the nib.
- Space toilets suck waste away with air, rather than flushing it away with water.

Astronaut food

Read each caption below, then number it to match the right picture.

☐ **Sealed drink pouches** prevent liquids from escaping when an astronaut has a drink.

☐ **Dried foods** need water added before they can be eaten.

☐ **Dried fruits** are taken from the packet one at a time, so they do not float away.

☐ **Cereals** are vacuum-packed. Astronauts add water, then suck up the cereal.

1

2

3

4

True or false?

Read the statements below, then check the boxes to show whether they are true or false. Use the information on this page and page 13 to help you.

	TRUE	FALSE
1. Astronauts train for space travel in water tanks.	☐	☐
2. Space toilets blow waste away.	☐	☐
3. To stop food and drinks from floating away, they are kept in sealed containers.	☐	☐
4. Astronauts are weightless in space because they are "falling" in orbit around Earth.	☐	☐
5. Astronauts are strapped into their sleeping bags to sleep so that they do not snore.	☐	☐
6. Astronauts have to exercise in space to keep their muscles from wasting away.	☐	☐

Key Dates of Space Exploration

People have been recording their observations about the night sky for more than 5,000 years. Improved technologies, such as telescopes and space probes, have allowed astronomers to see farther than ever. Probes have visited every planet in the Solar System, plus comets and asteroids.

Complete the timeline

Use the charts at the end of the book to fill in the missing dates or other information on this timeline.

Galileo

Isaac Newton

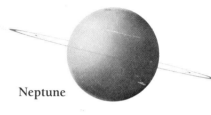
Neptune

928
Islamic astronomers perfect the astrolabe, an instrument that measures the position of the stars and planets.

1610
Italian scientist Galileo uses a telescope to discover the rings of ....

1687
English scientist Isaac Newton discovers the laws of gravity.

....
The outermost and windiest planet, Neptune, is discovered.

1926
American scientist Robert Goddard launches the first liquid-fuel rocket.

Space shuttle *Columbia*

First use of a Manned Maneuvering Unit (MMU)

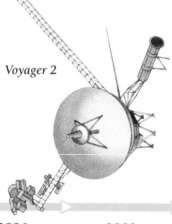
Voyager 2

Hubble Space Telescope

1981
The first reusable space vehicle, US space shuttle *Columbia*, is launched.

1984
US astronaut .... uses an MMU to make the first untethered spacewalk.

1986
The US space probe *Voyager 2* arrives at Uranus after making flybys of Jupiter and Saturn.

1989
The US *Voyager 2* probe makes the first flyby of Neptune.

1990
The Hubble Space Telescope is launched by the space shuttle *Discovery*.

1995
Valeri Poliakov completes .... days on board the space station *Mir*— the longest stay in space.

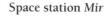
Space station *Mir*

Sputnik 1

Yuri Gagarin

Neil Armstrong

Venera 9

1957

The space race begins when the Soviet Union launches the first artificial satellite, *Sputnik 1*.

....

Yuri Gagarin is the first person in space. He orbits Earth in the Soviet spacecraft *Vostok 1*.

1962

The US space probe *Mariner 2* becomes the first probe to reach another planet, Venus.

1969

US astronaut Neil Armstrong becomes the first person on the ....

1971

The Soviet Union launches the first space station, *Salyut 1*. It orbits Earth for six months.

1975

The Soviet space probe *Venera 9* transmits the first images from the surface of the planet Venus.

International Space Station (ISS)

Mars rover

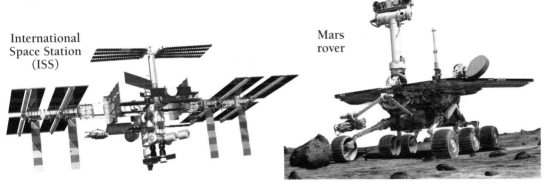

New Horizons

2000

A Russian *Soyuz* spacecraft carries the first crew to the ISS—two Russians and an American.

2003

China launches its first manned spacecraft, *Shenzhou 5*, with astronaut Yang Liwei on board.

2004

US rovers *Spirit* and *Opportunity* explore the surface of Mars.

2005

US space probe *Deep Impact* deliberately collides with the comet Tempel 1.

2011

Launch of the last space shuttle, on a supply mission to the ISS

2015

The US space probe *New Horizons* flies past Pluto and its moon Charon.

Deep Impact

Discovering the Universe

Check or number the boxes to answer each question. Check your answers on page 46.

1 Astronomers measure distances in space using:

- ☐ **a.** light days
- ☐ **b.** light kilometers
- ☐ **c.** light years
- ☐ **d.** light miles

2 Number these things 1 to 4 in order of size, starting with the biggest:

- ☐ **a.** galaxy
- ☐ **b.** Universe
- ☐ **c.** Solar System
- ☐ **d.** star

3 The Universe began:

- ☐ **a.** 14 thousand years ago
- ☐ **b.** 14 million years ago
- ☐ **c.** 14 billion years ago
- ☐ **d.** 14 trillion years ago

4 The Universe began in an explosion called the:

- ☐ **a.** Universal Explosion
- ☐ **b.** Big Explosion
- ☐ **c.** Big Crunch
- ☐ **d.** Big Bang

5 Number these events 1 to 5, starting with the earliest:

- ☐ **a.** The Universe began with the Big Bang.
- ☐ **b.** The oldest stars in the Milky Way were born.
- ☐ **c.** Our Solar System was formed.
- ☐ **d.** The first atoms began to form.
- ☐ **e.** Matter clumped together to form the first galaxies.

6 The Italian scientist Galileo used a telescope to discover the rings of:

- ☐ **a.** Mercury
- ☐ **b.** Mars
- ☐ **c.** Saturn
- ☐ **d.** Uranus

7 Which of these is *not* a good place for an observatory:

- ☐ **a.** high in the mountains
- ☐ **b.** away from populated areas
- ☐ **c.** out in space
- ☐ **d.** in a city

8 A telescope that focuses light waves is called:

- ☐ **a.** a digital telescope
- ☐ **b.** an optical telescope
- ☐ **c.** an X-ray telescope
- ☐ **d.** a radio telescope

9 Check all the types of rays that can be recorded by space observatories:

- ☐ **a.** X-rays
- ☐ **b.** sting rays
- ☐ **c.** gamma rays
- ☐ **d.** ultraviolet rays

10 A space probe is:

- ☐ **a.** a thermometer in Earth orbit
- ☐ **b.** a telescope in Earth orbit
- ☐ **c.** an unmanned spacecraft that investigates space
- ☐ **d.** a manned spacecraft

Stars, Galaxies, and Constellations

Check or number the boxes to answer each question. Check your answers on page 46.

1 Stars are mainly made up of:

- ☐ **a.** hydrogen
- ☐ **b.** oxygen
- ☐ **c.** carbon dioxide
- ☐ **d.** rock

2 Check all the colors that stars can be:

- ☐ **a.** yellow
- ☐ **b.** blue
- ☐ **c.** green
- ☐ **d.** red

3 The cloud of gas and dust from which a star forms is called a:

- ☐ **a.** nebula
- ☐ **b.** galaxy
- ☐ **c.** black hole
- ☐ **d.** comet

4 Number these captions 1 to 6 to show the life cycle of a small star like our Sun:

- ☐ **a.** Nuclear reactions in the core produce heat and light.
- ☐ **b.** The outer layers of gas puff out like a ring of smoke to form a planetary nebula.
- ☐ **c.** When the star is cold and stops glowing, it forms a black dwarf.
- ☐ **d.** The star runs low on fuel, and expands into a red giant.
- ☐ **e.** The star is born in a nebula (a cloud of dust and hydrogen gas).
- ☐ **f.** The faint remains of the star become a white dwarf.

5 A constellation is a:

- ☐ **a.** group of stars that are very close to each other
- ☐ **b.** vast, spinning group of stars, gas, and dust
- ☐ **c.** group of stars that make a pattern in the sky

6 How many constellations do astronomers divide the sky into?

- ☐ **a.** 22
- ☐ **b.** 44
- ☐ **c.** 66
- ☐ **d.** 88

7 Check all the things that are constellations:

- ☐ **a.** Ursa Major
- ☐ **b.** Pole Star
- ☐ **c.** Cassiopeia
- ☐ **d.** Southern Cross

8 Which of these is *not* a type of galaxy?

- ☐ **a.** spiral
- ☐ **b.** cuboid
- ☐ **c.** elliptical
- ☐ **d.** oval

9 How many galaxies are there in the part of the Universe we can observe?

- ☐ **a.** 100 thousand
- ☐ **b.** 100 million
- ☐ **c.** 100 billion
- ☐ **d.** 100 trillion

10 Our home galaxy is called:

- ☐ **a.** the Milky Galaxy
- ☐ **b.** the Milky Way
- ☐ **c.** the Solar Galaxy
- ☐ **d.** the Solar System

11 How long does it take the Sun to orbit the center of our galaxy:

- ☐ **a.** 225 years
- ☐ **b.** 225 thousand years
- ☐ **c.** 2.25 million years
- ☐ **d.** 225 million years

Planets and Smaller Space Bodies

Check or number the boxes to answer each question. Check your answers on page 46.

1 Check all the different types of planets:

☐ **a.** smooth
☐ **b.** rocky
☐ **c.** gas
☐ **d.** metal

2 The clump of matter from which a planet forms is called a:

☐ **a.** protoplanet
☐ **b.** miniplanet
☐ **c.** potential planet
☐ **d.** nebula

3 Check all the rocky planets:

☐ **a.** Earth
☐ **b.** Jupiter
☐ **c.** Mars
☐ **d.** Mercury
☐ **e.** Neptune
☐ **f.** Saturn
☐ **g.** Uranus
☐ **h.** Venus

4 Craters are made on a planet's surface by:

☐ **a.** meteorites (space rocks) bombarding the planet
☐ **b.** spacecraft landing on the planet
☐ **c.** volcanic eruptions
☐ **d.** huge storms

5 Gas planets have a core made of:

☐ **a.** dust
☐ **b.** liquid
☐ **c.** iron
☐ **d.** rock

6 Check all the things found in the rings around the gas planets:

☐ **a.** rock
☐ **b.** ice
☐ **c.** metal
☐ **d.** gas

7 A natural object that orbits a planet is called its:

☐ **a.** ring
☐ **b.** asteroid
☐ **c.** moon
☐ **d.** meteorite

8 Where is the asteroid belt?

☐ **a.** between the Sun and Mercury
☐ **b.** between Earth and Mars
☐ **c.** between Mars and Jupiter
☐ **d.** beyond Neptune

9 A comet's glowing tail is released when:

☐ **a.** the comet burns up in the Earth's atmosphere
☐ **b.** a nuclear reaction takes place inside the comet
☐ **c.** the comet heats up as it nears the Sun

10 A shooting star is:

☐ **a.** a star falling to Earth
☐ **b.** a meteor burning up as it enters Earth's atmosphere
☐ **c.** another name for a comet
☐ **d.** an asteroid exploding

The Sun and Solar System

Check or number the boxes to answer each question. Check your answers on page 46.

1 The Sun's energy comes from:

- [ ] **a.** burning hydrogen gas on its surface
- [ ] **b.** giant volcanoes all over its surface
- [ ] **c.** nuclear reactions inside its core

2 Check all the things that are part of the Sun:

- [ ] **a.** core
- [ ] **b.** prominence
- [ ] **c.** corona
- [ ] **d.** crust

3 How long does the Sun's equator take to rotate once?

- [ ] **a.** 25 Earth hours
- [ ] **b.** 25 Earth days
- [ ] **c.** 34 Earth hours
- [ ] **d.** 34 Earth days

4 The hottest part of the Sun is:

- [ ] **a.** its sunspot
- [ ] **b.** its surface
- [ ] **c.** its atmosphere
- [ ] **d.** its core

5 Number the planets of the Solar System 1 to 8, starting with the planet that is nearest to the Sun:

- [ ] **a.** Earth
- [ ] **b.** Mars
- [ ] **c.** Mercury
- [ ] **d.** Jupiter
- [ ] **e.** Neptune
- [ ] **f.** Saturn
- [ ] **g.** Uranus
- [ ] **h.** Venus

6 How big is the Solar System?

- [ ] **a.** 9,300 billion miles (15,000 billion km) across
- [ ] **b.** 9.3 billion miles (15 billion km) across
- [ ] **c.** 9,300 miles (15,000 km) across

7 A planet's year is:

- [ ] **a.** the amount of time it takes the Sun to orbit it once
- [ ] **b.** the amount of time it takes to orbit the Sun once
- [ ] **c.** the amount of time it takes to spin once on its axis

8 Which is the hottest planet in the Solar System?

- [ ] **a.** Jupiter
- [ ] **b.** Mercury
- [ ] **c.** Saturn
- [ ] **d.** Venus

9 Which of these planets is *not* visible with the naked eye?

- [ ] **a.** Mercury
- [ ] **b.** Saturn
- [ ] **c.** Uranus
- [ ] **d.** Venus

10 Check all the things that are features of Mars:

- [ ] **a.** Great Red Spot
- [ ] **b.** Valles Marineris
- [ ] **c.** Olympus Mons
- [ ] **d.** Kuiper Belt

11 Which of these planets has seven rings?

- [ ] **a.** Jupiter
- [ ] **b.** Saturn
- [ ] **c.** Uranus
- [ ] **d.** Neptune

Earth and the Moon

Check or number the boxes to answer each question. Check your answers on page 46.

1 Which of these space bodies is *not* smaller than Earth?

- ☐ **a.** Jupiter
- ☐ **b.** Moon
- ☐ **c.** Mars
- ☐ **d.** Venus

2 Earth's orbit around the Sun is elliptical. This means:

- ☐ **a.** diamond-shaped
- ☐ **b.** oval-shaped
- ☐ **c.** circular
- ☐ **d.** square-shaped

3 How long does it take for the Earth to rotate on its axis?

- ☐ **a.** 23 hours 56 minutes
- ☐ **b.** 12 hours
- ☐ **c.** 365.26 days
- ☐ **d.** 12 months

4 How much of Earth's surface is covered in water?

- ☐ **a.** 60 percent
- ☐ **b.** 70 percent
- ☐ **c.** 80 percent
- ☐ **d.** 90 percent

5 Check all the words that describe the Earth's core:

- ☐ **a.** hot
- ☐ **b.** cold
- ☐ **c.** solid
- ☐ **d.** iron

6 The Moon is kept in Earth's orbit by:

- ☐ **a.** energy from the Sun
- ☐ **b.** magnetism
- ☐ **c.** gravity
- ☐ **d.** nuclear power

7 The Moon's light comes from:

- ☐ **a.** nuclear reactions within its core
- ☐ **b.** reflected light from the Sun
- ☐ **c.** its burning hot surface
- ☐ **d.** its radioactive surface

8 Number these captions 1 to 5 to show what happens in a solar eclipse:

- ☐ **a.** After a few minutes, the dark circle begins to move off the Sun.
- ☐ **b.** An hour later, the eclipse is over.
- ☐ **c.** The Moon appears to take a bite out of the Sun as it starts to pass in front of it.
- ☐ **d.** All of the Moon is in front of the Sun. The Sun's corona shines around the Moon's dark circle.
- ☐ **e.** Over the course of about an hour, the Moon covers more and more of the Sun.

9 Which of these is *not* one of the Moon's phases?

- ☐ **a.** Full Moon
- ☐ **b.** New Moon
- ☐ **c.** Blue Moon
- ☐ **d.** waning gibbous

10 During a lunar eclipse, the Moon may glow:

- ☐ **a.** red
- ☐ **b.** yellow
- ☐ **c.** blue
- ☐ **d.** violet

Astronauts and Spacecraft

Check or number the boxes to answer each question. Check your answers on page 46.

1 Number these landmarks of space exploration 1 to 6, starting with the earliest:

- ☐ **a.** first person on the Moon
- ☐ **b.** first space station
- ☐ **c.** first liquid-fuel rocket
- ☐ **d.** first artificial satellite
- ☐ **e.** first untethered spacewalk
- ☐ **f.** first person in space

2 In order to burn its fuel, a space rocket must carry a supply of:

- ☐ **a.** oxygen
- ☐ **b.** carbon dioxide
- ☐ **c.** matches
- ☐ **d.** wood

3 Check all the space bodies on which astronauts have landed:

- ☐ **a.** Moon
- ☐ **b.** Mars
- ☐ **c.** Jupiter
- ☐ **d.** Venus

4 A vehicle that can travel on the surface of another planet is called a:

- ☐ **a.** wanderer
- ☐ **b.** rover
- ☐ **c.** voyager
- ☐ **d.** spacecar

5 Which of these was *not* a space shuttle orbiter?

- ☐ **a.** Discovery
- ☐ **b.** Endeavour
- ☐ **c.** Apollo
- ☐ **d.** Atlantis

6 Which part of the space shuttle could *not* be reused?

- ☐ **a.** winged orbiter
- ☐ **b.** twin booster rockets
- ☐ **c.** external fuel tank
- ☐ **d.** mechanical arm

7 How many astronauts have traveled beyond Earth's orbit?

- ☐ **a.** 3
- ☐ **b.** 11
- ☐ **c.** 24
- ☐ **d.** over 400

8 Astronauts on board spacecraft have to exercise regularly because:

- ☐ **a.** their bodies are weighed down in space and their joints may ache
- ☐ **b.** weightlessness means they can't sit down, so their legs ache
- ☐ **c.** they do not get enough food, so they become tired easily
- ☐ **d.** weightlessness means their bodies do not work so hard and their muscles could waste away
- ☐ **e.** they need to be strong to open the airlock and carry out spacewalks

9 Check all the things that a spacesuit must supply:

- ☐ **a.** food
- ☐ **b.** water
- ☐ **c.** oxygen
- ☐ **d.** electrical supply

10 In a spacecraft, food is kept in sealed containers so that:

- ☐ **a.** mice cannot eat it
- ☐ **b.** it does not float away
- ☐ **c.** it does not rot
- ☐ **d.** the astronauts don't eat too much

Activity Answers

Once you have completed each page of activities,
check your answers below:

Page 14
Watching the night sky
1 b
2 c
3 a
4 d

Page 14
How a telescope works
1 mirrors
2 light rays
3 reflects
4 eyepiece
5 lens

Page 15
Light years away
1 50,740 billion miles
   (81,700 billion km)
2 1,829,000 billion miles
   (2,945,000 billion km)
3 217,120 billion miles
   (349,600 billion km)
4 149,270 billion miles
   (240,350 billion km)

Page 15
Star colors
1 O
2 yellow
3 9,000°F (5,000°C)
4 O, B, A, F

Page 16
Star knowledge
1 10
2 red giant
3 has stopped glowing
4 supernovas

Page 17
The Milky Way in numbers
1 100,000
2 100 billion
3 225 million
4 500,000 mph (800,000 kph)
5 200 billion

Page 17
Spot the galaxy
1 spiral galaxy
2 elliptical galaxy
3 irregular galaxy

Page 18
Northern polar stars
1 b
2 d
3 a
4 e
5 c

Page 19
Southern polar stars
1 e
2 d
3 c
4 b
5 a

Page 20
Parts of the Sun

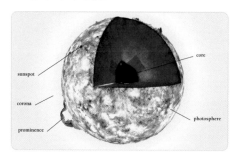

Page 20
True or false?
1 True
2 False—The Earth and other planets
   orbit the Sun.
3 False—The Sun is a giant ball of
   hydrogen gas.
4 False—Sunspots are cooler than the
   rest of the Sun's surface.
5 True

Page 21
Orbiting objects
Moon: (nothing)
Earth: Moon, space station, satellite
Sun: planets, Earth

Page 21
Birth of the Solar System
a 3
b 4
c 2
d 1

Page 22
Planets of the Solar System
1 Neptune
2 Mercury
3 Saturn
4 Earth
5 Uranus
6 Venus
7 Jupiter
8 Mars

Page 22
Planet puzzles
1 Neptune
2 84 Earth years
3 59 Earth days
4 Mercury and Venus

Page 23
Earth time teasers
1 7
2 100

Page 24
Mercury or Venus?
1 Venus
2 Mercury
3 Venus
4 Venus
5 Venus

Page 25
Earth from space

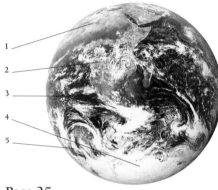

Page 25
Earth challenge
1 iron
2 Sun
3 atmosphere
4 icecaps
5 landmasses

Page 27
Eclipse in action
1 The Moon appears to take a bite out of the Sun as it starts to pass in front of it.
2 Over the course of about an hour, the Moon covers more and more of the Sun.
3 All of the Moon is in front of the Sun. The Sun's corona shines around the Moon's dark circle.
4 After a few minutes, the dark circle begins to move off the Sun.
5 An hour later, the eclipse is over.

Page 28
Mars in close-up
1 c
2 d
3 b
4 a

Page 29
Gas planet puzzle
1 Great Red Spot
2 Uranus
3 gas and liquid
4 Uranus

Page 30
Planet names puzzle
1 Jupiter
2 Mars
3 Mercury
4 Neptune
5 Saturn
6 Uranus
7 Venus

Page 30
Planet challenge
1 Jupiter
2 Mercury and Venus
3 Neptune
4 Saturn
5 Neptune

Page 31
Small space bodies
1 dwarf planet
2 meteorites
3 meteors
4 Comet
5 asteroid belt
6 meteorites

Page 32
After the Big Bang
1 Big Bang
2 atoms
3 galaxies
4 Milky Way
5 Solar System

Page 33
Into orbit and back again

1 The orbiter's main engines and rocket boosters fired together at liftoff.

2 Two minutes after liftoff, the rocket boosters fell back to Earth.

3 Eight minutes after takeoff, the external fuel tank dropped away.

4 The orbiter remained in orbit for up to two weeks.

5 Protective silica tiles glowed as the orbiter reentered the atmosphere.

6 The orbiter glided in to land on an ordinary runway.

Page 33
Parts of the orbiter

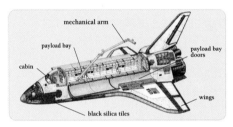

mechanical arm
payload bay
payload bay doors
cabin
wings
black silica tiles

Page 34
Astronaut suit
1 undersuit
2 boots
3 outersuit
4 helmet
5 gloves
6 visor

Page 34
Astronauts at work
1 science
2 astronauts
3 oxygen
4 cosmonauts

Page 35
Astronaut food
1 Dried foods
2 Cereals
3 Dried fruits
4 Sealed drink pouches

More answers on next page

Page 35
True or false?
1 True
2 False—Space toilets suck waste away.
3 True
4 True
5 False—Astronauts are strapped into their sleeping bags so that they do not float around the spacecraft.
6 True

Page 36
1846 The outermost and windiest planet, Neptune, is discovered.

1984 US astronaut Bruce McCandless uses an MMU to make the first untethered spacewalk.

1995 Valeri Poliakov completes 437 days on board the space station *Mir*—the longest stay in space.

Page 37
1961 Yuri Gagarin is the first person in space. He orbits Earth in the Soviet spacecraft *Vostok 1*.

1969 US astronaut Neil Armstrong becomes the first person on the Moon.

Quick Quiz Answers

Once you have completed each page of quiz questions, check your answers below:

Page 38
Discovering the Universe
1 c 2 a2, b1, c3, d4 3 c 4 d
5 a1, b4, c5, d2, e3 6 c 7 d 8 b
9 a, c, d 10 c

Page 39
Stars, Galaxies, and Constellations
1 a 2 a, b, d 3 a
4 a2, b4, c6, d3, e1, f5 5 c 6 d
7 a, c, d 8 b 9 c 10 b 11 d

Page 40
Planets and Smaller Space Bodies
1 b, c 2 a 3 a, c, d, h 4 a 5 d 6 a, b
7 c 8 c 9 c 10 b

Page 41
The Sun and Solar System
1 c 2 a, b, c 3 b 4 d
5 a3, b4, c1, d5, e8, f6, g7, h2 6 a
7 b 8 d 9 c 10 b, c 11 b

Page 42
Earth and the Moon
1 a 2 b 3 a 4 b 5 a, c, d 6 c 7 b
8 a4, b5, c1, d3, e2 9 c 10 a

Page 43
Astronauts and Spacecraft
1 a4, b5, c1, d2, e6, f3 2 a 3 a 4 b
5 c 6 c 7 c 8 d 9 b, c, d 10 b

Acknowledgments

The publisher would like to thank the following:

Alyson Silverwood for proofreading, Ian Ridpath for 2020 consultant review, and Harish Aggarwal, and Priyanka Sharma for the jacket.

The publisher would like to thank the following for their kind permission to reproduce their photographs:

(Key: a-above; b-below/bottom; c-center; f-far; l-left; r-right; t-top)

3 NASA: ESA / NASA / SOHO (cla); JPL / Cornell University (crb). 6 Dorling Kindersley: Anglo-Australian Observatory (cla). 7 Getty Images: Photodisc / StockTrek (cra). NASA: ESA / NASA / SOHO (bl). 8 Dorling Kindersley: NASA / JPL (tr). NASA: JPL / Space Science Institute (crb). 9 Dorling Kindersley: NASA (cr). 10 Dreamstime.com: Reinhold Wittich (cb). NASA: JPL-Caltech / T. Pyle (SSC) (bc). 11 Dorling Kindersley: (cb). NASA: JPL (cra). 12 Dorling Kindersley: NASA (cr). NASA: (br); JPL / Cornell University (ca). 13 NASA: (cla, cr, cb, br). 14 Dorling Kindersley: Anglo-Australian Observatory / David Malin (cra). Dreamstime.com: Dymon / Dmitry Volkov (cl). ESO: D. Baade/https:// creativecommons.org/licenses/by/4.0 (cra/ moon). 17 Canada-France-Hawaii Telescope: J.-C. Cuillandre / Coelum (bc/M87). NASA: ESA / Hubble & NASA; Acknowledgement: Judy Schmidt (bc); (br). 21 Getty Images: 500px / Wojtek Miś (cl). NASA: ESA / NASA / SOHO (c); JPL-Caltech / T. Pyle (SSC) (cb). 22 Dorling Kindersley: NASA (cr). 22-23 NASA: ESA / NASA / SOHO (c). 23 Dorling Kindersley: © The Trustees of the British Museum. All rights reserved. (bl). 25 NASA: (cra). 26 Science Photo Library: Eckhard Slawik (cra). 27 Dorling Kindersley: NASA (clb). 28 Dorling Kindersley: NASA (br). NASA: JPL-Caltech ©. 30 Dorling Kindersley: © The Trustees of the British Museum. All rights reserved. (cr). Getty Images: Bettmann (clb). 31 NASA: (ca). 32 123RF.com: Andrey Alyukhin (cl/explosion). NASA: JPL-Caltech / T. Pyle (SSC) (bl). 35 NASA: (bl). 36 Dorling Kindersley: (crb); NASA (fclb). Dreamstime.com: Georgios Kollidas (ca). NASA: (clb). 37 Getty Images: Bettmann (cla). NASA: (ca, crb); JPL / Cornell University (cb); JPL-Caltech / UMD (bc). 38 Dorling Kindersley: Anglo-Australian Observatory (cra). NASA: ESA / NASA / SOHO (crb). 39 NASA: ESA / STScI / J. Hester and P. Scowen (Arizona State University) (cra). 42 Dorling Kindersley: (ca, cl); NASA (clb). 43 Dorling Kindersley: NASA (ca, cb). NASA: (cl). 45 NASA: (cla).

All other images © Dorling Kindersley
For further information see:
www.dkimages.com

SOLAR SYSTEM FACTS

Name	Mercury (planet)	Venus (planet)	Earth (planet)
Distance from Sun	36 million miles (57.9 million km)	67.2 million miles (108.2 million km)	92.9 million miles (149.6 million km)
Period of Revolution	88 Earth days	224.7 Earth days	365.26 Earth days
Equatorial Diameter	3,029 miles (4,875 km)	7,521 miles (12,104 km)	7,926 miles (12,756 km)
Moons	0	0	1

Name	Mars (planet)	Jupiter (planet)	Saturn (planet)
Distance from Sun	141.6 million miles (227.9 million km)	483.6 million miles (778.3 million km)	888 million miles (1.43 billion km)
Period of Revolution	687 Earth days	11.86 Earth years	29.46 Earth years
Equatorial Diameter	4,213 miles (6,780 km)	88,846 miles (142,984 km)	74,898 miles (120,536 km)
Moons	2	79	53 known, 29 unconfirmed

Name	Uranus (planet)	Neptune (planet)	Pluto (dwarf planet)
Distance from Sun	1.78 billion miles (2.87 billion km)	2.8 billion miles (4.5 billion km)	3.7 million miles (5.9 billion km)
Period of Revolution	29.46 Earth years	29.46 Earth years	29.46 Earth years
Equatorial Diameter	31,763 miles (51,118 km)	31,763 miles (49,532 km)	1,432 miles (2,304 km)
Moons	27	14	5

Name	Ganymede (Jupiter's Moon)	Titan (Saturn's Moon)	Moon (Earth's Moon)
Distance from Sun	664,470 miles (1.07 million km)	758,000 miles (1.22 million km)	238,900 miles (384,400 km)
Period of Revolution	7.15 Earth days	15.95 Earth days	27.3 Earth days
Equatorial Diameter	3,267 miles (5,262 km)	3,200 miles (5,150 km)	2,160 miles (3,476 km)
Moons	0	0	0

SPACE RECORD-BREAKERS

RECORD	FIRST PERSON IN SPACE	FIRST WOMAN IN SPACE	FIRST SPACE WALK
STATISTICS	ORBITED EARTH IN VOSTOK 1	71-HOUR FLIGHT ON VOSTOK 6	24 MINUTES OUTSIDE VOSKHOD 2
NAME	YURI GAGARIN	VALENTINA TERESHKOVA	ALEXEI LEONOV
ORIGIN	SOVIET UNION	SOVIET UNION	SOVIET UNION
YEAR	1961	1963	1969

RECORD	FIRST PERSON ON MOON	FIRST UNTETHERED SPACE WALK	LONGEST STAY IN SPACE
STATISTICS	SPENT A TOTAL OF 22 HOURS ON MOON SURFACE	USED A MANNED MANEUVERING UNIT (MMU) OUTSIDE CHALLENGER	437 DAYS ON BOARD MIR
NAME	NEIL ARMSTRONG	BRUCE MCCANDLESS	VALERI POLIAKOV
ORIGIN	USA	USA	RUSSIA
YEAR	1969	1984	1994–1995

RECORD	FASTEST ORBITING PLANET	HOTTEST PLANET	LARGEST PLANET RINGS
NAME	MERCURY	VENUS	SATURN
STATISTICS	ORBITS SUN AT 29.8 MILES/SECOND (47.9 KM/SECOND)	AVERAGE SURFACE TEMPERATURE 867°F (464°C)	RING WIDTH 170,000 MILES (275,000 KM)
FEATURES	ROCK AND METAL	ROCK AND METAL	ICE AND DUST
DISCOVERY	PLANET DISCOVERED IN ANCIENT TIMES	PLANET DISCOVERED IN ANCIENT TIMES	RINGS DISCOVERED IN 1610

RECORD	MOST FREQUENT COMET	LARGEST ASTEROID	WINDIEST PLANET
NAME	ENCKE	CERES	NEPTUNE
STATISTICS	RETURNS TO INNER SOLAR SYSTEM EVERY 3.3 YEARS	DIAMETER 596 MILES (960 KM)	WIND SPEEDS 1,340 MPH (2,160 KPH)
FEATURES	ICE AND ROCK	ROCK	WATER, METHANE, AND AMMONIA ICE
DISCOVERY	COMET DISCOVERED IN 1786	ASTEROID DISCOVERED IN 1801	PLANET DISCOVERED IN 1846